Table of Contents

Introduction
Recipes Included in This Book
Pizza Recipes
Garlic Chicken Pizza
High Protein Thin-Crust Pizza
Hearty Vegetable Pizza
New York Pizza
Spinach and Mushroom White Pizza
Easy Garlic and Cheese Pizza Thins
Three Cheese Buffalo Pizza
Chicken Pesto Pizza
Tex-Mex Pizza
Veggie Hummus Pizza
Southwest Avocado Pizza
Baked BLT
Fontina and Arugula Pizza
Cheesy Artichoke Pizza
Spinach and Mushroom Pizza
Onion and Gorgonzola Pizza
Summer Veggies and Ranch Pizza
Sausage Pizza
Two-Step Pizza DoughHerbed Pizza Crust

Introduction

There's no shortage of things to love about pizza—from the crisp or tender crust, bubbling sharp cheese, hearty vegetables and succulent meats. It's no wonder you, like most, have your favorite pizzeria on speed dial—despite the fact that making your own pizza at home is now easier than ever.

Imagine this—not only can you use sauce that is tailor fit to your palate, you can also make your pizza crust as thin or as thick as you like, as crisp or tender and you prefer, topped with vegetables and meats that you know you will eat and combine various cheeses that are meant to satisfy your craving. This recipe book will get you started on the basics—simple but gourmet-quality pizzas that you can enjoy at home. But when you do, be sure to keep these guidelines in mind:

- Pre-heat your oven before popping your pizza in. This will ensure that your pizza cooks evenly and perfectly.
- Pre-heat oven at a high heat—anywhere from 400-475 degrees should work.
- Place pizza at the center of the oven racks to distribute heat evenly.
- This goes without saying, but please be reminded that pizza baking in the oven is piping hot. And when you're ready to pull it out of the oven, be sure to use oven mitts to protect yourself.
- Allow your pizza to cool before cutting it. If the pizza is too hot, a less than samurai-sharp pizza cutter will just cause your cheese to get caught in the blade and ruin your entire pizza.
- While cooling, let it rest on a wooden board or dish towel.
- Pizza is cooked when the cheese has melted and has just begun to brown around the edges. The crust should be a medium golden brown hue.
- If you're using store bought pizza crust, make sure you season it well with herbs and spices of your choice.
- Grease your baking pan with olive oil to keep the crust from sticking. This also allows the crust to absorb a little flavor and adds depth to your pizza.

- If you're making your own dough, roll from the center so that it spreads evenly.
- Use a toothpick to poke small holes in the crust so that it doesn't bubble in just one area.
- Go easy on the sauce to keep your pizza from getting soggy.
- Pizza stores great in the freezer. Assemble your pizza, wrap tightly in cling film and pop in the freezer. Defrost overnight in the refrigerator and bake in the oven once you're ready to enjoy it.

The great thing about making pizza at home is that you can customize it whatever way you want. And in no time, you won't need to call your trusty pizza delivery.

Delicious Pizza Recipes

Recipes Included in This Book

Garlic Chicken Pizza

High Protein Thin-Crust Pizza

Hearty Vegetable Pizza

New York Pizza

Spinach and Mushroom White Pizza

Easy Garlic and Cheese Pizza Thins

Three Cheese Buffalo Pizza

Chicken Pesto Pizza

Tex-Mex Pizza

Veggie Hummus Pizza

Southwest Avocado Pizza

Baked BLT

Fontina and Arugula Pizza

Cheesy Artichoke Pizza

Spinach and Mushroom Pizza

Onion and Gorgonzola Pizza

Summer Veggies and Ranch Pizza

Sausage Pizza

Two-Step Pizza Dough
Herbed Pizza Crust

Pizza Recipes

Garlic Chicken Pizza

Prep Time: 35 minutes

Servings: 6

Ingredients:

1 14" premade pizza crust

1 cup cornmeal

1 cup Parmesan cheese and roasted garlic sauce

1/4 teaspoon granulated garlic

2 cups mozzarella cheese, shredded

2 grilled skinless, boneless chicken breasts, diced

1/4 red onion, sliced

1 tomato, cut into thin wedges

1 green bell pepper, seeded and diced

1 cup cilantro, finely chopped

Directions:
1. Set oven to 475 degrees.
2. Sprinkle cornmeal on pizza crust and pat into place.
3. Spread sauce on top and top with all remaining ingredients evenly.
4. Bake for 20-25 minutes until cheese is melted.

High Protein Thin-Crust Pizza

Prep Time: 35 minutes

Servings: 6-8

Ingredients:

2 pounds ground beef

1 pound pepperoni, sliced thinly

1/2 pound bacon, chopped

2 teaspoons salt

1 pinch cayenne pepper

1 pinch ground black pepper

2 cups tomato sauce

1 18" premade pizza crush, rolled thin

1 1/2 cup mozzarella cheese

Directions:

1. Set oven to 475 degrees.
2. Spread sauce on dough and top with all remaining ingredients evenly.
3. Bake for 15-20 minutes until cheese is melted.

Hearty Vegetable Pizza

Prep Time: 30 minutes

Servings: 2

Ingredients:

1 18" premade pizza crust

Sauce:

1 can diced tomatoes

1 can tomato paste

1/2 small onion, chopped

1 tablespoon dried oregano

1 clove garlic, finely chopped

1 teaspoon onion powder

1 teaspoon kosher salt

1 pinch ground black pepper

Toppings:

1 1/4 cups shredded mozzarella cheese

1/2 cup chopped green bell pepper

1/2 cup chopped onion

1/2 cup sliced fresh mushrooms

Directions:

1. Set oven to 475 degrees.
2. In a sauce pan, bring all sauce ingredients to a slow simmer.
3. Spread sauce on dough and top with all remaining ingredients evenly.
4. Bake for 20-25 minutes until cheese is melted.

New York Pizza

Prep Time: 35 minutes

Servings: 4

Ingredients:

1 14" premade pizza crust

6 ounces mozzarella cheese, thinly sliced

1/2 cup canned crushed tomatoes

1/4 teaspoon freshly ground black pepper

1/2 teaspoon dried oregano

3 tablespoons extra-virgin olive oil

6 leaves fresh basil, torn

Directions:

1. Set oven to 475 degrees.
2. Spread tomatoes and sauce on dough and top with all remaining ingredients evenly.
3. Bake for 20-25 minutes until cheese is melted.

Spinach and Mushroom White Pizza

Prep Time: 35 minutes

Servings: 10-14

Ingredients:

1 bunch frozen chopped spinach, thawed and drained

1 bottle premade Alfredo sauce

1 can sliced mushrooms, drained

1/2 cup grated Parmesan cheese

4 cups shredded mozzarella cheese

2 14" premade pizza crusts

2 tablespoons butter, softened

Directions:
1. Set oven to 475 degrees.
2. Spread Alfredo sauce on dough and top with all remaining ingredients evenly.
3. Divide softened butter between assembled pizzas.
4. Bake for 20-25 minutes until cheese is melted.

Easy Garlic and Cheese Pizza Thins

Prep Time: 15 minutes

Servings: 2-4

Ingredients:

2 12" flour tortillas

1 cup low-fat mayonnaise

1 cup mozzarella cheese

1/2 cup Parmesan cheese

1/2 cup garlic, finely chopped

1/2 cup cilantro, finely chopped

Directions:

1. Set oven to 475 degrees.
2. Spread mayonnaise on flour tortillas and top with cheese evenly.
3. Sprinkle with cilantro and cheese
4. Bake for 10 minutes until cheese is melted and flour tortillas are crisp.

Three Cheese Buffalo Pizza

Prep Time: 40 minutes

Servings: 6

Ingredients:

3 chicken breast halves, cooked, skinned, deboned and cubed

2 tablespoons butter, melted

1 cup garlic and herbs pizza sauce

1 bottle hot sauce

1/2 cup blue cheese, crumbled

1 16" premade pizza crust

1 cup mozzarella cheese, shredded

1 cup Colby Jack cheese, shredded

Directions:

1. Combine butter and hot sauce together. Toss chicken pieces with the buffalo sauce.
2. Set oven to 475 degrees.
3. Spread sauce on dough and top with all remaining ingredients, including chicken cubes, evenly.
4. Bake for 20-25 minutes until cheese is melted.

Chicken Pesto Pizza

Prep Time: 35 minutes

Servings: 6

Ingredients:

1/2 cup pesto basil sauce

1 12" premade pizza crust

2 cups chicken breasts, sliced into strips

1 jar artichoke hearts, drained

1/2 cup mozzarella cheese, shredded

1/2 cup parmesan cheese, grated

Directions:

1. Set oven to 475 degrees.
2. Spread pesto on dough and top with all remaining ingredients evenly.
3. Bake for 20-25 minutes until cheese is melted.

Tex-Mex Pizza

Prep Time: 45 minutes

Servings: 10-14

Ingredients:

1 can tomato paste

3/4 cup water

1 package taco seasoning mix

1 teaspoon chili powder, or to taste

1/2 teaspoon cayenne pepper, or to taste

1 can refried beans

1/3 cup salsa

1/4 cup chopped onion

1/2 pound ground beef

4 cups shredded Cheddar cheese

2 12" premade pizza crusts

Directions:

1. Set oven to 475 degrees.
2. Whisk tomato paste and water with taco seasoning mix and chili powder and cayenne pepper in a sauce pan.
3. Spread sauce on dough and top with all remaining ingredients evenly.
4. Bake for 20-25 minutes until cheese is melted.

Veggie Hummus Pizza

Prep Time: 35 minutes

Servings: 4-6

Ingredients:

1 14" premade pizza crust

1 cup hummus spread

1 1/2 cups sliced bell peppers

1 cup broccoli florets

2 cups shredded Monterey Jack cheese

Directions:

1. Set oven to 475 degrees.
2. Spread hummus on dough and top with all remaining ingredients evenly.
3. Bake for 20-25 minutes until cheese is melted.

Southwest Avocado Pizza

Prep Time: 35 minutes

Servings: 4-8

Ingredients:

2 avocados, peeled, pitted and diced

1 tablespoon cilantro, finely chopped

1 tablespoon fresh lime juice

Salt and pepper, to taste

1 clove garlic, finely chopped

4 8" premade pizza crusts

1 tablespoon olive oil

1 cup chicken breasts, cooked and chopped

1 cup cherry tomatoes, quartered

1 cup Monterey Jack cheese, shredded

1 pinch cayenne pepper

1 cup pizza sauce

Directions:

1. Set oven to 475 degrees.
2. Spread sauce on each pizza crust and top with all remaining ingredients evenly.
3. Bake for 20-25 minutes until cheese is melted.

Baked BLT

Prep Time: 35 minutes

Servings: 6

Ingredients:

4 slices bacon

1 10" premade pizza crust

1 teaspoon olive oil

2 cups mozzarella cheese, shredded

1 tomato, chopped

2 cups shredded iceberg lettuce

2 tablespoons mayonnaise, or to taste

Salt and pepper to taste

Directions:

1. Set oven to 475 degrees.
2. Spread mayonnaise on pizza crust and top with all remaining ingredients evenly.
3. Bake for 20-25 minutes until cheese is melted.

Fontina and Arugula Pizza

Prep Time: 35 minutes

Servings: 6

Ingredients:

1 12" inch premade pizza crust

6 tablespoons prepared pesto sauce

3 Roma tomatoes, thinly sliced

1 jar seasoned fontina cheese, crumbled

2 cloves garlic, peeled and thinly sliced

1 cup fresh arugula, torn

1 teaspoon olive oil

Directions:

1. Set oven to 475 degrees.
2. Spread pesto sauce on pizza crust and top with all remaining ingredients evenly.
3. Bake for 20-25 minutes until cheese is melted.

Cheesy Artichoke Pizza

Prep Time: 35 minutes

Servings: 6

Ingredients:

1 14" premade pizza crust

1/2 cup Alfredo sauce

1 small jar marinated artichoke hearts, drained and roughly chopped

1 medium tomato, cut in half and sliced

2 cloves garlic, finely chopped

1 cup Colby-Monterey Jack cheese, shredded

1 cup mozzarella cheese, shredded

Directions:

1. Set oven to 475 degrees.
2. Spread sauce on pizza crust and top with all remaining ingredients evenly.
3. Bake for 20-25 minutes until cheese is melted.

Spinach and Mushroom Pizza

Prep Time: 30 minutes

Servings: 6

Ingredients:

1 12" premade pizza crust

1 cup pizza sauce

3 tablespoons olive oil

1 teaspoon sesame oil

1 cup fresh spinach, rinsed and dried

8 ounces shredded mozzarella cheese

1 cup assorted mushrooms, sliced

Directions:

1. Set oven to 475 degrees.
2. Spread olive oil and pizza sauce on pizza crust and top with all remaining ingredients evenly.
3. Bake for 20-25 minutes until cheese is melted.

Onion and Gorgonzola Pizza

Prep Time: 35 minutes

Servings: 4-6

Ingredients:

1/8 cup butter

2 large onions, thinly sliced

2 teaspoons sugar

1 10" premade pizza crust

1 pound Gorgonzola cheese, crumbled

Directions:

1. Set oven to 475 degrees.
2. Spread butter on pizza crust and top with all remaining ingredients evenly.
3. Bake for 20-25 minutes until cheese is melted.

Summer Veggies and Ranch Pizza

Prep Time: 35 minutes

Servings: 6-8

Ingredients:

1 18" premade pizza crust

1 1/2 cups Ranch-style salad dressing

2 cups shredded Cheddar cheese

1/2 cup shredded carrots

1/2 cup chopped cauliflower

1/2 cup chopped fresh broccoli

1/2 cup chopped onion

1/2 cup chopped red bell pepper

1/2 cup sliced fresh mushrooms

1 pound mozzarella cheese, shredded

Directions:

1. Set oven to 475 degrees.
2. Spread ranch dressing on pizza crust and top with all remaining ingredients evenly.
3. Bake for 20-25 minutes until cheese is melted.

Sausage Pizza

Prep Time: 35 minutes

Servings: 6

Ingredients:

1 package Italian sausage links, casings removed

1 12" premade pizza crust

1 cup pizza sauce

1 1/4 cups shredded mozzarella cheese, divided

1/2 cup chopped green peppers

Directions:

1. Preheat oven to 475 degrees.
2. Spread sauce on pizza crust and top with all remaining ingredients evenly.
3. Bake for 20-25 minutes until cheese is melted.

Two-Step Pizza Dough

Prep Time: 35 minutes

Servings: 6-12

Ingredients:

3 cups all-purpose flour

1 (.25 ounce) package active dry yeast

2 tablespoons vegetable oil

1 teaspoon salt

1 tablespoon white sugar

1 cup warm water (45 degrees C)

Directions:

1. Mix flour, sugar, salt and yeast in a large mixing bowl. Add oil and warm water.
2. Spread into a pizza pan—choose a smaller pan for a thicker crust or a larger one for a thinner crust. Bake at 375 degrees for 20-25 minutes.

1.

Herbed Pizza Crust

Prep Time: 35 minutes

Servings: 6-12

Ingredients:

1 package active dry yeast

1 cup herbs of choice

1 teaspoon white sugar

1 cup warm water (45 degrees C)

2 1/2 cups bread flour

2 tablespoons olive oil

1 teaspoon salt

Directions:

1. Mix flour, sugar, salt and yeast in a large mixing bowl. Add oil, warm water and fresh herbs.
2. Spread into a pizza pan—choose a smaller pan for a thicker crust or a larger one for a thinner crust. Bake at 375 degrees for 20-25 minutes.

Printed in Great Britain
by Amazon